SMART ABOUT
History

SMART ABOUT THE

PRESIDENTS

Written and illustrated by
Jon Buller & Susan Schade,
Maryann Cocca-Leffler,
Dana Regan,
and Jill Weber

Grosset & Dunlap ★ New York

For Mr. Streb—J.B. & S.S.

To my daughters and girls everywhere who aspire to be president—M.C-L.

To Joe and Tommy, who may grow up to be president one day—D.R.

To R, O, J&J—J.W.

The following pages are copyright © 2004 Jon Buller and Susan Schade: p. 11 Thomas Jefferson; p. 16 Martin Van Buren; p. 21 Millard Fillmore; p. 25 Andrew Johnson; p. 30 Grover Cleveland (first term); p. 31 Benjamin Harrison; p. 36 Woodrow Wilson; p. 40 Franklin D. Roosevelt; p. 42 D.D. Eisenhower; p. 45 Richard Nixon; p. 48 Ronald Reagan; p. 56 Vice Presidents; p. 57 First Ladies; p. 60 Can a President Get Fired?; p. 61 Presidents in Retirement

The following pages are copyright © 2004 Maryann Cocca-Leffler: p. 6 Who Can Be President?; p. 8 The Presidential Oath of Office; p. 9 George Washington; p. 13 James Monroe; p. 17 William H. Harrison; p. 26 Ulysses S. Grant; p. 32 Grover Cleveland (second term); p. 37 Warren Harding; p. 38 Calvin Coolidge; p. 43 John F. Kennedy; p. 47 Jimmy Carter; p. 49 George Bush; pp. 54–55 The White House

The following pages are copyright © 2004 Dana Regan: p. 7 What Is the Job, Exactly?; p. 10 John Adams; p. 14 John Quincy Adams; p. 19 James K. Polk; p. 22 Franklin Pierce; p. 23 James Buchanan; p. 27 Rutherford B. Hayes; p. 34 Theodore Roosevelt; p. 35 William H.Taft; p. 39 Herbert Hoover; p. 41 Harry S. Truman; p. 46 Gerald Ford; p. 51 George W. Bush; p. 58 The Presidents' Kids; p. 59 Why It's Fun to Be President

The following pages are copyright © 2004 Jill Weber: front cover; back cover; title page; p. 2 spot art; p. 4 kids' letter; p. 5 lettering; p. 12 James Madison; p. 15 Andrew Jackson; p. 18 John Tyler; p. 20 Zachary Taylor; p. 24 Abraham Lincoln; p. 28 James Garfield; p. 29 Chester A. Arthur; p. 33 William McKinley; p. 44 Lyndon B. Johnson; p. 50 Bill Clinton; p. 52 2004 Election Winner; p. 53 2004 Election Loser; pp. 62–63 Where Were the Presidents Born?; p. 64 spot for Bibliography

All rights reserved. Published by Grosset & Dunlap, a division of Penguin Young Readers Group, 345 Hudson Street, New York, New York 10014. GROSSET & DUNLAP is a trademark of Penguin Group (USA) Inc. Manufactured in China.

Library of Congress Cataloging-in-Publication Data

Smart about the presidents / written and illustrated by Jon Buller . . . [et al.].
    v. cm. — (Smart about history)
  Includes bibliographical references (p.).
  Contents: Who can be president? – What is the job, exactly? – The presidential oath of office – The presidents – 2004 election winner – 2004 election loser – The White House – Vice presidents – First ladies – The presidents' kids – Why it's fun to be president – Can a president get fired? – Presidents in retirement – Where were the presidents born?
  ISBN 0-448-43372-9 (pbk.)
  1. Presidents–United States–Juvenile literature. [1. Presidents.] I. Buller, Jon, 1943– II. Series.
  E176.1.S618 2004
  973'.09'9–dc22   2003022559

ISBN 0-448-43372-9   10 9 8 7 6 5 4 3 2 1

From the desk of

Ms. Brandt

Dear Class,

   I am so eager to see your group reports. I hope that working together with classmates will be lots of fun. It's very different from doing a report all by yourself, isn't it?
   First your group needs to pick a subject. Then you must figure out a way to divide the work fairly. And <u>then</u> you have to put the whole report together.
   This is not an easy assignment. But I know that you will all do a GREAT job!

Ms. Brandt

About This Report

Dear Ms. Brandt,

We decided to do our class report on the presidents. Because we all wanted to do the same presidents (like Abraham Lincoln and George Washington), we picked presidents' names from a hat.

Besides learning about the presidents, we also did research on the White House and first ladies and kids of the presidents.

It was really interesting. When we were all done, we celebrated with vanilla ice cream with blueberries and strawberries—a red, white, and blue treat!

Team West Wing   Lucy   Ori

Maria   Ethan   Tommy

P.S. Pages 52 and 53 are for *you* to fill out after we know who wins the next presidential election.

P.P.S. After doing our report, we all decided one thing. Nobody wants to be vice president!

 Table of Contents

Who can be PRESIDENT?

The U.S. Constitution says that the president of the United States must be:

★ born in the United States

★ at least 35 years old

★ a United States citizen and must have lived in the U.S. for at least 14 years

I'm going to be the first woman president!

future first brother

future White House pet

What Is The Job, Exactly?

Our government has three branches. The judicial branch includes all of the federal courts, all the way to the Supreme Court. The legislative branch passes laws and is made up of the House of Representatives and the Senate. The executive branch is the president, the vice president, and the people the president appoints to give him advice (the cabinet).

The president tries to get laws passed in Congress. He can also veto (say no to) laws that he doesn't agree with. The president is also the commander of all the armed forces and he can declare war with the approval of Congress. Here are some other things the president does:

He nominates Supreme Court justices and other important judges.

He negotiates treaties with other governments.

He appoints U.S. ambassadors to foreign countries.

He can pardon anyone convicted of a federal crime.

THE PRESIDENTIAL OATH of Office

Every president has taken the same oath.

I do solemnly swear that I will faithfully execute the office of the President of the United States, and will, to the best of my ability, preserve, protect, and defend the Constitution of the United States.

PRESIDENT George Washington ★ 1

From 1789 to 1797

Born in Virginia, George Washington was the most famous hero of the Revolutionary War. When the war was over, it was time for the new nation (now called the United States of America) to pick its first leader. Everyone wanted George Washington. But nobody knew what to call him! Finally, the decision was made to call our top leader "president." And that's how it's been ever since.

Father of our country

Your Elective Majesty?

King?

Your High Mightiness?

President?

Mmm. "President" sounds good.

Feb. 22, 1732 – Dec. 14, 1799

He loved animals and his staff brushed his horse's teeth every day! George Washington wore false teeth that some books say were made of animal bone and tusk.

The father of our country had no children of his own. He married Martha Custis and adopted her two children.

Before he was president: He was a farmer and surveyor (someone who measures land).

Did you know this? George Washington was the only president who never lived in the White House.

(It wasn't finished being built.)

★2 PRESIDENT John Adams

From 1797 to 1801

Declaration of Independence

John Adams helped Thomas Jefferson write the Declaration of Independence. Our second president died 50 years after the birthday of the U.S. on July 4, 1826—the exact same day as Thomas Jefferson. John and his wife Abigail were the first residents in the White House.

Oct. 30, 1735–
July 4, 1826

Home
Sweet
Home

Abigail Adams hung laundry in the unfinished East Room of the White House.

Before he was president: He was George Washington's vice president. He hated the job!

Did you know this? His son John Quincy Adams became president.

Good job, son!

Thanks, Dad!

10

PRESIDENT Thomas JEFFERSON ⭐3

From 1801 to 1809

Jefferson was probably the smartest president ever. He was interested in everything—like science and art and music and farming and language and law and government.
When he was president, he bought over 600 million acres of land (called the Louisiana Purchase) from France. This made the United States twice as big as it was before. And all that land only cost three cents an acre.

JEFFERSON'S HOME WAS CALLED MONTICELLO. HE DESIGNED IT HIMSELF.

April 13, 1743 – July 4, 1826

THE LOUISIANA PURCHASE

ZAT WILL BE $15 MILLION.

NO PROBLEM!

NAPOLEON

DEED $3

DICK, HIS PET MOCKINGBIRD, TOOK FOOD FROM HIS LIPS.

Before he was president: Thomas Jefferson

wrote the Declaration of Independence.

Did you know this?   Jefferson invented

a folding ladder, and collected prehistoric bones.

 **4** PRESIDENT James **Madison**

From **1809** to **1817**

I was the first president to wear long pants.

Constitution of the United States
We the people

March 16, 1751 – June 28, 1836

Before he became president, James Madison helped write the Constitution and the Bill of Rights. The Constitution explains how our government works. The Bill of Rights says what we are free to do as citizens. Did you know he was the shortest president, only five feet, four inches tall and 100 pounds? His wife, Dolley, was one of the most popular first ladies ever.

British soldiers set fire to the White House during the War of 1812.

Dolley managed to save the famous portrait of George Washington.

HA, HA!

Before he was president: James Madison was a lawyer, congressman, and secretary of state.

Did you know this?

Francis Scott Key wrote "The Star-Spangled Banner" in 1814.

PRESIDENT James Monroe 5

From 1817 to 1825

James Monroe left college at 17 to join General George Washington's army and fight the British. During the Revolutionary War, he was shot. The bullet stayed in his shoulder for the rest of his life. When he first became president, the White House was being rebuilt after the fire, so Monroe toured the country for four months. He was the first president to travel around greeting the people.
A smart and popular president, Monroe is best known for the Monroe Doctrine, which told European countries to keep their hands off the New World!

April 28, 1758 ~ July 4, 1831

Monroe's daughter Maria was the first child of a president to be married in the White House.

Monroe
wife, Elizabeth
daughter, Eliza

He was the third president who died on the fourth of July.

Senator
Governor
Minister to Britain, France, and Spain
Secretary of State
Secretary of War

Before he was president: Monroe held more major offices than any other president.

Did you know this? Monroe was the first president to travel on a steamship.

In 1819 the first American steamship crossed the Atlantic.

It had sails!

6 PRESIDENT John Quincy Adams

From 1825 to 1829

Smile!

I am smiling.

He was the first president to have his picture taken.

July 11, 1767 – Feb. 23, 1848

In the presidential election of 1824, none of the candidates won a majority of the electoral votes. The winner was decided by the House of Representatives, which chose Adams. Like his father, who was president before him, John Quincy Adams got on many people's nerves. He didn't like being president and when he didn't win a second term, he ran for Congress and spent 17 years there.

When he was president, John Quincy Adams would swim naked in the Potomac River most mornings.

No peeking!

Before he was president: John Quincy Adams had many jobs in government. When he was 11, he was his father's secretary in France

Did you know this? He loved to garden.

PRESIDENT Andrew Jackson

From 1829 to 1837

Andrew Jackson became a soldier when he was only 13. Both his parents were dead by the time he was 14. He sure had to grow up fast! Before he became president, he fought in two wars—the Revolutionary War and the War of 1812. Thanks to Andrew Jackson, the White House got bathrooms and running water. Here is a weird fact: he insisted the world was flat.

Andrew Jackson was the first president born in a log cabin.

They called me Old Hickory because I was tough as wood.

IT'S FLAT!

March 15, 1767–June 8, 1845

Oh, my!

*@!x!*0!

Jackson's pet parrot had to be taken away at his funeral because it was swearing.

Before he was president: Andrew Jackson was a lawyer, judge, military governor of Florida, U.S. senator, and congressman.

Did you know this? In 1829 the typewriter was invented.

In 1836 Davy Crockett fought the Mexicans at the Alamo. & Arkansas became the 25th state.

15

PRESIDENT Martin VAN BUREN

I'M "O.K."

Dec. 5, 1782 - July 24, 1862

From 1837 to 1841

As soon as Martin Van Buren became president, the United States started going through some tough times. People lost their jobs and didn't have enough money for food and rent. It was Van Buren's idea for the government to have its own treasury, instead of keeping its money in private banks. The law for this was passed in 1840, just before his term as president ended. He ran for a second term, but he lost to William Henry Harrison.

GOOD IDEA, MARTIN!

U.S. TREASURY

THANKS!

FAMILY: WIFE, HANNAH, AND FOUR SONS

Before he was president: He had lots of jobs in the government — senator, governor of New York, secretary of state, and vice president.

Did you know this? He came from Kinderhook, N.Y., and his nickname was Old Kinderhook — O.K. for short.

PRESIDENT William H. Harrison 9

From Mar. 4, 1841 to April 4, 1841

Here's the long and the short of it: William Henry Harrison is known for having the shortest presidential term in history . . . because he gave the longest inauguration speech in history! He talked for one hour and 40 minutes and caught a cold that turned into pneumonia. He died after spending just 32 days in office! Not much happened in the short time he was president.

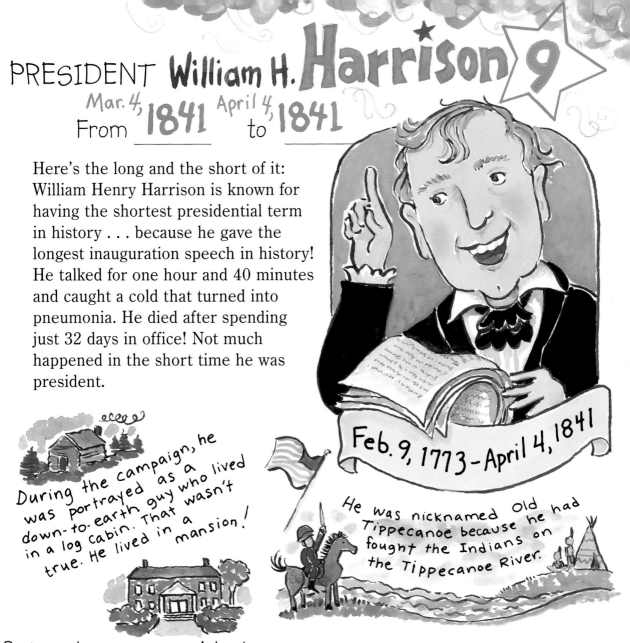

Feb. 9, 1773 – April 4, 1841

During the campaign, he was portrayed as a down-to-earth guy who lived in a log cabin. That wasn't true. He lived in a mansion!

He was nicknamed Old Tippecanoe because he had fought the Indians on the Tippecanoe River.

Before he was president: He went to medical school to be a doctor. After his father died, he quit and joined the army.

Did you know this? He married Anna Symmes and had ten kids and 48 grandkids, one of whom (Benjamin) became our 23rd president.

PRESIDENT John Tyler

From 1841 to 1845

Vice president John Tyler became president after President Harrison died in office. He was playing marbles with his kids when he found out the news.

People nicknamed Tyler "His Accidency," and didn't want him to make decisions like a real president. But he did anyway! When it was time for the next election, Tyler wasn't nominated.

I am too the real president!

Mar. 29, 1790–Jan. 18, 1862

Our father had 15 children! That's the most of any president.

1ST WIFE: Letitia   2nd WIFE: Julia

Pets: Johnny Ty   The General   Le Beau

Before he was president: John Tyler was a lawyer, governor of Virginia, U.S. senator, and congressman.

Did you know this?

In 1845 Florida became the 27th state.

In 1845 there was a potato famine in Ireland. Many Irish people started coming to America.

PRESIDENT James K. POLK

From 1845 to 1849

Polk didn't trust banks. He hid all his money at home.

Nov. 2, 1795 – June 15, 1849

President Polk believed the United States should expand westward to the Pacific Ocean. This idea is called Manifest Destiny. While he was president, the U.S. had the biggest increase in size since Jefferson's presidency. Polk tried to buy land from Mexico, but when Mexico refused, Polk went to war. The U.S. defeated Mexico, and gained California and New Mexico.

President Polk and his wife Sarah hosted the first formal Thanksgiving dinner ever served at the White House.

Before he was president: He was governor of Tennessee.

Did you know this? Polk and his wife were good friends with Francis Scott Key who wrote "The Star-Spangled Banner."

oh, say can you see...

PRESIDENT Zachary Taylor
From 1849 to 1850

I was smart but a terribul speller.

Nov. 24, 1784 – July 9, 1850

Zachary Taylor was elected president because he had been a great military leader. As president, he tried to keep the North and South from fighting. In the White House, he wore farm clothes instead of getting dressed up. And he chewed tobacco! He was president for only 16 months. The story is that he got sick and died after eating cherries and iced milk at a July fourth party.

OUCH!

Whitey, his horse, grazed on the White House lawn till people yanked hairs from his tail as souvenirs.

Wife, Margaret, and four kids

Before he was president: Zachary Taylor was a soldier in the war of 1812 and a general in the Mexican War.

Did you know this?

1849 THE GOLD RUSH BEGAN

Safety pin invented in 1849

1849 Harriet Tubman escaped slavery by travelling on the Underground Railroad to the North.

PRESIDENT Millard FILLMORE

From 1850 to 1853

The California gold rush had just started when Vice President Fillmore became president. Thousands of people travelled to California hoping

GOLD!

to find gold and get rich. Fillmore gave government money to build a railroad from the East Coast all the way to the West Coast, and bring back the gold. After his term was up, he ran for president on his own, but he lost. His wife, Abigail, had been a schoolteacher. She started the White House library.

BORN IN LOG CABIN

Jan. 7, 1800 - March 8, 1874

CALIFORNIA OR BUST!

Before he was president: He was a teacher, a lawyer, a state assemblyman, and a U.S. congressman.

Did you know this? When he was 19, he was a student in the class of his future wife, Abigail.

1+1=2

PRESIDENT Franklin **Pierce**

From 1853 to 1857

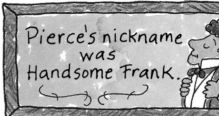

Pierce's nickname was Handsome Frank.

Nov. 23, 1804 – Oct. 8, 1869

As president, Franklin Pierce tried to keep the peace between the Northern states and the Southern states. The Kansas-Nebraska Act was passed in 1854. It said that these two territories would vote to decide whether to allow slavery or not. This did not solve the problem and our country headed closer to war.

Pierce liked to drive his carriage very fast. Once, he knocked a woman over and he was arrested.

Stop, Mr. President!

Before he was president: Franklin Pierce was a senator from New Hampshire when he was only 32 years old.

Did you know this? His 11-year-old son died in a train accident just weeks before Pierce became president.

PRESIDENT James Buchanan ⭐ 15

From 1857 to 1861

Buchanan was the first president to have a royal guest stay at the White House. (It was England's Prince Albert.)

James Buchanan was the only president who never got married. The girl he loved broke off their engagement after an argument. He was very unhappy the whole time he was in office and glad he only served one term. A former lawyer, he argued that slavery was legal and hoped the two sides of the issue would reach a compromise. They didn't.

April 23, 1791 – June 1, 1868

We're leaving!

In February 1861 seven Southern states formed the Confederate States of America. Four more (Virginia, North Carolina, Tennessee, and Arkansas) joined later.

Before he was president: He was the minister to Russia and to Britain, a senator, and secretary of state.

Did you know this? Buchanan's niece Harriet Lane served as the hostess for his White House.

PRESIDENT Abraham Lincoln

From 1861 to 1865

I liked to keep important papers in my hat.

Feb. 12, 1809 – April 15, 1865

Abraham Lincoln was very poor growing up and lived in a log cabin. He couldn't go to school often, but he loved to read. He was president during the Civil War when the North and South were fighting against each other. Five days after the South surrendered, President Lincoln was shot while he was at the theater. He died the next morning. He was one of our greatest presidents ever.

TALLEST PRESIDENT

6'4"

No shave, please.

First president to have a beard

BOB

We're Nano and Nanko.

I'm Jack and that's Jib.

PETS

FIRST LADY MARY

He loved playing with his younger sons, who both died when they were very young.

Before he was president: Abraham Lincoln was a storekeeper, a rail-splitter, a postmaster, and a lawyer.

Did you know this?

LINCOLN MADE THE LAST THURSDAY OF NOVEMBER THE OFFICIAL THANKSGIVING DAY.

PRESIDENT Andrew JOHNSON

From 1865 to 1869

Andrew Johnson started out as a tailor in Greeneville, Tennessee. Then he got into politics and eventually became vice president under Abraham Lincoln. After Lincoln was shot, Andrew Johnson became president. He disagreed with Congress about lots of things and Congress tried to throw him out of office through an impeachment. They couldn't do it, so he stayed. But he was president for only one term. On page 60, you can find out how a president can get fired.

THIS IS HOW I GOT MY START!

Dec. 29, 1808 – July 31, 1875

I'M NOT GOING!

DURING JOHNSON'S PRESIDENCY, THE U.S. BOUGHT ALASKA FROM RUSSIA FOR $7 MILLION.

SOME DEAL!

Before he was president: After they were married, Johnson's wife helped teach him to write.

P IS FOR PRESIDENT!

Did you know this? He was the only president who became a U.S. senator after he left the White House.

PRESIDENT **Ulysses S. Grant**

From <u>**1869**</u> to <u>**1877**</u>

His real name was Hiram Ulysses Grant.

During the Civil War, General Ulysses S. Grant helped lead the North to victory. When he ran for president, he won easily. Unfortunately, many of the men he appointed lied, cheated, and took bribes. Later, Grant lost all his savings. To make sure he left his family with money, he wrote a book about his life. It became a best-seller.

About me

HERO

April 27, 1822 – July 23, 1885

He once got a $20 speeding ticket for driving too fast in Washington, D.C.

In 1872 he created the first national park, Yellowstone.

He married Julia Dent and had four children. Mrs. Grant loved to entertain. One dinner party at the White House had 29 courses.

Before he was president: <u>He was a store clerk and soldier.</u>

Did you know this? <u>In 1872 Grant was the first president to run against a woman.</u>

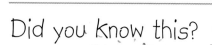
Vote for me!

Victoria Woodhull
(She lost.)

PRESIDENT Rutherford B. Hayes ★19

From 1877 to 1881

Hayes was the first president to use a telephone in the White House.

Hello?

In the 1876 presidential race, Congress had to recount the vote. Right before inauguration day, Hayes was declared the winner. Lots of voters were very angry and said he hadn't won. They called him Ruther*fraud* B. Hayes. He kept his campaign promise and did not run for re-election.

Oct. 4, 1822–
Jan. 17, 1893

First Lady Lucy Hayes hosted the first Easter Egg Roll on the White House lawn in 1878.

Before he was president: He was a general in the Union Army during the Civil War.

Did you know this? His wife became known as Lemonade Lucy because she did not serve any liquor at White House parties.

Lemonade   3¢

PRESIDENT James A. Garfield

From 1881 to 1881

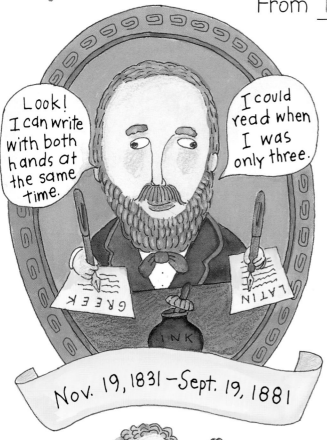

Look! I can write with both hands at the same time.

I could read when I was only three.

GREEK

LATIN

INK

Nov. 19, 1831 – Sept. 19, 1881

James A. Garfield didn't believe in giving people government jobs just as a favor. (Some other presidents used to do this.) A crazy man who didn't get the job he wanted shot him. At first it seemed as if President Garfield would recover, but after several months, he died.

He was the second president to be assassinated.

FIRST LADY

LUCRETIA

KIDS

VETO

GARFIELD JUGGLED CLUBS FOR EXERCISE.

Before he was president: James A. Garfield was the

⭐ ⭐ ⭐ only president who was a preacher.

Did you know this?

1881 CLARA BARTON FOUNDED ➕ THE AMERICAN RED CROSS

1881

GUNFIGHT AT THE OK CORRAL

PRESIDENT Chester A. Arthur

From 1881 to 1885

Chester A. Arthur became president after President Garfield was assassinated. Like Garfield, President Arthur wanted to make the government more honest—some of his old friends who wanted jobs were mad about that. People called him Elegant Arthur, because he loved fancy clothes. He had more than 80 pairs of pants!

I WAS ONE OF THE BEST FISHERMEN IN AMERICA.

Oct. 5, 1829–Nov. 18, 1886

His sister Mary acted as the first lady because his wife had died.

MARY

KIDS

GOOD BANJO PLAYER!

Before he was president: Chester A. Arthur was a teacher, lawyer, and the vice president.

Did you know this?

1883 FINISHED

THE BROOKLYN BRIDGE

1882 New York City got electricity.

1885

THE ADVENTURES OF HUCKLEBERRY FINN BY MARK TWAIN

PRESIDENT Grover **CLEVELAND**

From <u>1885</u> to <u>1889</u> (FIRST TERM)

WILL YOU BE MINE, FRANCES?

I WILL, GROVER.

March 18, 1837 - June 24, 1908

PETS - HUNTING DOGS

BOOM

In the second year of his first term, he got married to Frances Folsom. She was a lot more beautiful than Grover, and 27 years younger. At 21, she was the youngest first lady ever, and became very popular. Cleveland was known for being honest. In 1888 he lost the election to Benjamin Harrison. (But you have not heard the last of Grover Cleveland.)

GROVER CLEVELAND WAS THE ONLY PRESIDENT TO GET MARRIED IN THE WHITE HOUSE.

Before he was president: He was a lawyer, the mayor of Buffalo, and the governor of New York.

Did you know this? When he was 17, Grover's dad died, and he had to quit school to support his family. Later, he went back to school.

PRESIDENT Benjamin HARRISON

From 1889 to 1893

Benjamin Harrison was the grandson of William Henry Harrison, the ninth president. Benjamin was a smart man and a good lawyer, but he wasn't a very successful or popular president. He didn't win a second term. During his presidency the Oklahoma Territory, which was supposed to be for Native Americans, was opened to white settlers, and there was a huge land rush.

August 20, 1833 – March 13, 1901

CHARGE!

FREE LAND

YAHEE!

THE OKLAHOMA LAND RUSH

Before he was president: He was a general in the Civil War.

Did you know this? Benjamin Harrison and his grandfather, William Henry Harrison, both kept pet goats.

24 PRESIDENT Grover CLEVELAND

From 1893 to 1897 (2nd term)

He answered his own phone!

I'm back!

Baby Ruth candy bar was named after Cleveland's daughter Ruth.

March 18, 1837 - June 24, 1908

It's Grover Cleveland again! He was the first and only president to serve two terms that were not in a row. He was an honest and hardworking president. Sometimes, he was still at his desk at two o'clock in the morning. His second term didn't go as well as his first. The country was in a Depression set off by the Great Panic of 1893. Banks and businesses closed and millions of people were out of work.

His daughter Esther was the only child of a president to be born in the White House.

ZZZZZ

When the Clevelands left the White House after the first term, his wife Frances said to the staff, "Take care of the furniture, we will be back in four years." She was right!

Pullman Strike
In 1894 railroad workers went on strike, affecting the entire country. Cleveland sent in troops to break up the strike.

STOP

Before he was president: He was president! (This was his second term!)

Did you know this? When Cleveland got drafted in the army during the Civil War, he paid someone to take his place. (At the time, that was legal!) He was needed at home to care for his mother.

PRESIDENT William McKinley 25

From 1897 to 1901

While William McKinley was president, the United States became a real world power. The country controlled lots of new territories like Guam, Puerto Rico, and the Philippines. And the United States also took over Hawaii. President McKinley loved inventions like the telegraph and the telephone. He was a very popular president. But during his second term, he was shot—the third president to be assassinated.

VOTE ★ FOR ★ McKINLEY

I was the first to use campaign buttons.

I always wore a red carnation for good luck!

Jan. 29, 1843–Sept. 14, 1901

First Lady Ida McKinley hated yellow.

Even the yellow roses were dug up at the White House.

FIRST PRESIDENT TO RIDE IN A CAR

Before he was president: McKinley was a county prosecutor, governor of Ohio, and congressman.

Did you know this?
First subway in the U.S. opened in 1897 in Boston.

Coca-Cola was invented in 1886 and then came Pepsi in 1898.

PRESIDENT Theodore Roosevelt

From 1901 to 1909

Oct. 27, 1858 – Jan. 6, 1919

Tennis, anyone?

Roosevelt was very athletic and loved sports.

Theodore Roosevelt was the vice president when William McKinley was assassinated. TR, as he was called, became the youngest president ever, at age 42. Roosevelt loved the outdoors and wanted to protect the environment for all Americans. He preserved millions of acres of national forest, established five national parks, and set up the first wildlife refuge.

Roosevelt and his six kids had fun in the White House. The children roller-skated in the halls and sledded down the stairs on cookie trays.

Before he was president: He was a writer, a cowboy, a hero of the Spanish-American War, and governor of New York.

Did you know this? The teddy bear is named after him.

PRESIDENT William H. Taft ⭐27

From **1909** to **1913**

Taft was the first president to buy a car for the White House.

Taft loved baseball. He started the tradition of presidents throwing out the first pitch on opening day. President Taft was easygoing and friendly, but he was not happy in his job. When he left the White House in 1913, he said it was "the lonesomest place in the world."

Sept. 15, 1857–
March 8, 1930

Taft needed a special bathtub installed in the White House, because he weighed more than 300 pounds. It was big enough to hold four men.

Before he was president: He was a lawyer and a judge.

Did you know this? After his presidency, Taft got his dream job. He became Chief Justice of the U.S. Supreme Court.

Order in the court!

28 PRESIDENT Woodrow WILSON

From 1913 to 1921

Dec. 28, 1856 – Feb. 3, 1924

WOODROW WILSON KEPT SHEEP ON THE WHITE HOUSE LAWN. ONE OF THEM, OLD IKE, LIKED TO CHEW TOBACCO.

1920: ALL WOMEN NOW GET TO VOTE

Woodrow Wilson liked being president. He tried to keep the U.S. out of World War I, but he couldn't do it. After the war, he helped to create the League of Nations, so that wars could be prevented in the future. He was disappointed when he couldn't convince Congress to let our country join the League of Nations.

Before he was president: He was a professor at Princeton, then the president of Princeton.

PRINCETON

Did you know this? After he was partly paralyzed by a stroke in 1919, his wife Edith had to help him with his duties as president.

PRESIDENT Warren G. Harding 29

From 1921 to 1923

Warren Harding was handsome and friendly, but he wasn't a very good president. When he was 19, he and two friends took over a newspaper in Marion, Ohio called the *Marion Star*. Through the newspaper, he met many important people who later steered him into politics. Soon, he was elected senator, then president. While in office, he surrounded himself with some very dishonest people. He died unexpectedly in office in 1923. After his death, many government scandals were uncovered.

Nov. 2, 1865 - Aug. 2, 1923

He liked playing golf more than being president.

☆ NEWS ☆
★ Warren Harding marries Florence Kling DeWolfe

They were not a happy couple and didn't have any children.

Harding had so many clothes that new closets had to be built in the White House.

President with the biggest feet — size 14!

Before he was president: He was a teacher, insurance salesman, newspaper editor, and senator.

Did you know this? Harding once gambled away a whole set of White House china.

In 1927, Coolidge congratulated Charles Lindbergh after he made the first solo flight across the

PRESIDENT Calvin Coolidge

From 1923 to 1929

A man of few words, he was known as Silent Cal.

July 4, 1872 – Jan. 5, 1933

Born on the fourth of July

Calvin Coolidge was vice president when President Harding died in office. In the middle of the night at his father's Vermont farm, he took the oath of office on the Coolidge family Bible. Frugal and honest, he cleaned up the scandals left from Harding's presidency and believed the less government, the better. Though quiet, he was a practical joker. Once, he rang for all the servants, then disappeared. He was the first president to hold regular press conferences.

"KEEP COOL-idge" was his campaign slogan. He was elected to a full term in 1924.

He married Grace Goodhue, who was a teacher of the deaf. Mrs. Coolidge once gave a speech entirely in sign language.

Coolidge exercised on an electric horse in the White House.

Before he was president: He was a farmer, lawyer, governor, and vice president.

Did you know this? Coolidge was an animal lover and had many exotic pets. His favorite was a pet raccoon, Rebecca.

PRESIDENT Herbert HOOVER ★ 31

From 1929 to 1933

Eight months after Hoover took office, the stock market crashed. Banks closed, businesses failed, and 13 million people were out of work by 1932. This was the time in history known as the Great Depression. Many people blamed Herbert Hoover for not doing enough to help the country out of the hard times. Homeless people lived in shantytowns called Hoovervilles. Herbert Hoover was not reelected.

Aug. 10, 1874-
Oct. 20, 1964

I'm hungry too.

Hoover promised voters "a chicken in every pot and a car in every garage," but then came the Great Depression.

Before he was president: He was a very successful businessman and a self-made millionaire.

Did you know this? He became an orphan at the age of nine.

From 1933 to 1945

FDR LOVED BOATS!

Jan. 30, 1882 – April 12, 1945

FDR, as he was called, was president longer than anyone. He was elected four times, and died in office just before World War II ended. He came from a rich family, but he wanted to help working people and poor Americans. He created lots of programs to help end the Great Depression of the 1930s, when millions of people were out of work.

FDR'S SCOTTISH TERRIER, FALA

FDR'S WIFE, ELEANOR, WOULD GO ANYWHERE TO TRY TO HELP POOR AND SICK PEOPLE.

Before he was president: When he was 39 years old, he got polio, and never recovered the use of his legs.

Did you know this? All through hard times FDR spoke to Americans in "fireside chats" on the radio.

THE ONLY THING WE HAVE TO FEAR IS FEAR ITSELF!

PRESIDENT Harry S. Truman 33

From 1945 to 1953

Hi, Bess!

Hi, Harry!

Truman met his wife, Bess, at Sunday school when he was six.

In 1945 President Franklin Roosevelt died in office and vice president Harry S. Truman became president. America was still fighting in WWII. Truman decided to drop two atomic bombs on Japan at Hiroshima and Nagasaki. The war ended soon after, but people still debate whether Truman was right to do this.

THE BUCK STOPS HERE

May 8, 1884 – Dec. 26, 1972

Truman loved to play piano.

Before he was president: He owned a men's clothing shop.

Did you know this? The "S" in his name doesn't stand for anything.

No, no, no.

Is it for Sidney?

Is it for Samuel?

Is it for Steven?

34 PRESIDENT Dwight David

From 1953 to 1961

Ike (that was Eisenhower's nickname) was a World War II hero because he led forces that won the war in Europe. The whole time he was president, there was a "cold war" going on between the U.S. and the USSR. A cold war is when there are no real battles, but each side tries to build more bombs and missiles than the other. The cold war didn't end until the 1990s. Ike liked golf and played it a lot.

Oct. 14, 1890 - March 28, 1969

IN THE 1950S, WHEN IKE WAS PRESIDENT, MORE PEOPLE THAN EVER BEFORE GOT TO LIVE THE AMERICAN DREAM, AND HAVE A JOB, A HOUSE, A CAR, AND A FAMILY.

IKE'S GRANDSON, DAVID, MARRIED RICHARD NIXON'S DAUGHTER, JULIE.

Before he was president: Ike was the president of Columbia University.

Did you know this? Ike's campaign slogan was "I Like Ike!"

PRESIDENT John F. Kennedy 35

From 1961 to 1963

America loved John F. Kennedy! At 43, he was the youngest person ever elected president. With his youth, charm, and style he represented the "new generation." He inspired young Americans to become volunteers in the Peace Corps, which he created in 1961. A WWII hero, Kennedy suffered with back pain from a war injury. On November 22, 1963 the entire country mourned after President Kennedy was shot and killed while riding in a Dallas parade.

"...ask not what your country can do for you; ask what you can do for your country."

First president who was a boy scout.

May 29, 1917 ~ Nov. 22, 1963

He married Jacqueline Bouvier, who brought beauty and glamour to the White House. She had her own sense of style and everyone wanted the "Jackie" look.

He supported the space program. Alan Shepard became the first American astronaut to rocket into space in 1961.

John F. Kennedy and Richard Nixon were the first presidential candidates to debate on TV. It helped Kennedy; he was handsome and witty.

Before he was president: He was a congressman, senator, and best-selling author.

Did you know this? In 1963 Martin Luther King Jr. gave his "I Have a Dream" speech in Washington, D.C.

PRESIDENT Lyndon B. Johnson

From 1963 to 1969

Everyone in our family has the same initials, LBJ, including Little Beagle Johnson.

Aug. 27, 1908 – Jan. 22, 1973

Lyndon B. Johnson took office after President Kennedy was assassinated. LBJ was a big man with a big personality. He liked to drive fast, and talk loud. He wanted the United States to be a "Great Society" and declared war on poverty. He created Medicare and Medicaid to help poor people and the elderly pay their doctor bills. He signed the Civil Rights Act of 1964 to make everyone equal. He won the 1964 election by a landslide. But the war in Vietnam turned people against him. He decided not to run again in 1968.

STOP THE WAR! PEACE NO WAR

FIRST LADY Lady Bird Johnson

Lynda Bird Johnson

Luci Baines Johnson

LBJ showed the world his scar.

Before he was president: LBJ was a teacher, rancher, U.S. senator, and vice president for JFK.

Did you know this?

1967 1st SUPER BOWL

1964 BEATLEMANIA

1968 Martin Luther King Jr. was assassinated

PRESIDENT Richard NIXON

From 1969 to 1974

Richard Nixon became president during the Vietnam War. He was elected two times. The second time, he won by a landslide. (That means a lot of votes.) But during the campaign, sneaky stuff was done. Men broke into Democratic Party headquarters in the Watergate building in Washington D.C. and were caught. It was a crime, and Nixon knew about it, but tried to cover it up. Because of the Watergate scandal, he became the only president to resign his job.

Jan. 9, 1913 - April 22, 1994

NIXON HAD A BOWLING ALLEY PUT INTO THE WHITE HOUSE.

DAUGHTERS TRICIA AND JULIE

WIFE PAT →

Before he was president: He was Ike's vice president. In 1960 he ran for president against Kennedy. They debated on TV.

DID TOO! DID NOT!

Did you know this? Nixon came back from World War II with poker winnings of more than $10 thousand.

PRESIDENT Gerald M FORD

From 1974 to 1977

The United States celebrated its 200th birthday while Ford was president

Gerald Ford became president in a very unusual way. He was never elected vice president or president, although he had both jobs. He was a congressman from Michigan when President Nixon appointed him vice president. Then, after President Nixon had to resign, Gerald Ford became President Ford. He ran for president in 1976, but lost to Jimmy Carter.

July 14, 1913-

Gerald Ford played football in college. He could have gone pro, but he went to Yale Law School instead.

Before he was president: He was a football coach and a model.

Did you know this? The Fords' daughter, Susan, had her senior prom in the White House.

PRESIDENT Jimmy Carter ⭐ 39

From 1977 to 1981

Jimmy Carter was humble, honest, and down-to-earth. That's just what the voters wanted after the Watergate scandal of the Nixon years. From peanut farmer to president, Carter was known as a peaceful leader. In 1978 he helped negotiate a peace treaty between Egypt and Israel, which was a high point in his presidency. A low point came when Americans were taken hostage in Iran. More than 50 were held for over a year and weren't released until the day Carter turned the presidency over to Ronald Reagan.

Oct. 1, 1924 ~

Carter's daughter, Amy, grew up in the White House. Carter built her a tree house on the White House lawn.

U.S.A. won't GO!

Carter ordered the U.S.A. to boycott the 1980 Summer Olympics in Moscow to protest the Soviet invasion of Afghanistan.

Carter was the first president to be born in a hospital. (The others were born at home.)

Future President

Before he was president: He was a peanut farmer, businessman, senator, and governor.

Did you know this? High oil prices of the 1970s caused the ENERGY CRISIS. Americans waited in long lines for gas.

GAS

PRESIDENT Ronald REAGAN

From 1981 to 1989

IN BEDTIME FOR BONZO, HE CO-STARRED WITH A CHIMPANZEE.

HIS FAVORITE CANDY WAS JELLY BEANS.

Feb. 6, 1911 -

Ronald Reagan is the only president who was an actor before he was in politics. Some of his most famous movies were *Knute Rockne: All American* and *Bedtime for Bonzo*. When he became president, he built up the Army, Navy, and Air Force. He also signed a treaty with the USSR to have fewer nuclear weapons. His policies were helpful in ending the cold war between the U.S. and the USSR.

WIFE #1 → ACTRESS JANE WYMAN
KIDS — MAUREEN AND MICHAEL

WIFE #2 → ACTRESS NANCY DAVIS
KIDS — PATTY AND RON

Before he was president: Ronald Reagan was governor of California.

Did you know this?

I WAS THE OLDEST PRESIDENT- ALMOST 70 WHEN I TOOK OFFICE.

I WAS THE YOUNGEST- 42 WHEN I TOOK OFFICE.

RONALD REAGAN →

← TEDDY ROOSEVELT

PRESIDENT George BUSH ⭐41

From 1989 to 1993

George Bush, at 19, was one of the youngest U.S. Navy pilots in WWII. On one mission, his plane was shot down over the South Pacific. He spent three hours in the shark-infested waters before he was rescued by a submarine! A graduate of Yale, he served as vice president for Ronald Reagan. A loyal family man, he thought of the White House as a "comfy family home" filled with grandchildren and pets. During his presidency, the cold war between the U.S. and the Soviet Union ended.

I hated broccoli and banned it from the White House.

June 12, 1924 -

Their dog Millie was the star of Millie's Book, written by Barbara Bush!

Bush, who lived in Texas, brought the game of horseshoes to the White House. He often played with his staff and groundskeepers.

Barbara Pierce was only 16 when she met George Bush. They married and had six children. Their oldest son went on to become our 43rd president.

Before he was president: He was a WWII pilot, Texas oilman, director of the CIA, and vice president.

Did you know this? In 1991 the U.S. declared war on Iraq to free Kuwait. This was known as the Gulf War.

PRESIDENT Bill Clinton

From 1993 to 2001

"I played the sax on T.V.!"

August 19, 1946—

Bill Clinton (his full name is William Jefferson Clinton) was the last president of the twentieth century. The 1990s were good years for the country—fewer people were out of work and the U.S. was not at war. Even after he lied about having an affair and was almost removed from office, Clinton remained a very popular president. He apologized to the American people and finished his second term.

Loves peanut butter & banana and FAST FooD

Clinton was allergic to Sox

AH CHOO

BUDDY

Chelsea, their daughter

First lady Hillary became a senator from New York

He jogged to keep off the fat.

Before he was president: Clinton was a lawyer, a law professor, and the governor of Arkansas.

He loved golf.

Did you know this?

Michael Jordan retires for the first time in 1993.

MILLION MAN MARCH 1995

MILLION MOM MARCH

Mother's Day 2000

PRESIDENT George W. Bush ⭐ 43

From **2001** to _____

Former president George Bush is George W. Bush's dad.

"Hi, # 43!"

"Hi, # 41!"

July 6, 1946-

The 2000 presidential election was very close. George W. Bush did not win the popular vote, just like Rutherford B. Hayes, Benjamin Harrison, and John Quincy Adams before him. The U.S. Supreme Court finally decided four weeks after the election that Bush was the winner. Eight months after he became president, a terrible thing happened. On September 11, 2001 New York City and Washington D.C. were attacked by terrorists. The U.S. went to war with Afghanistan in 2001. In 2003 the U.S. went to war against Iraq.

Bush and his wife Laura like to vacation on their ranch in Texas.

Before he was president: He was part-owner of the Texas Rangers baseball team.

Did you know this? George W. Bush was the first president to be elected in the twenty-first century.

51

CANDIDATE _____

Running Mate _____

WINNER 2004

POLITICAL PARTY

REPUBLICAN   circle one   DEMOCRAT

WRITE ABOUT THE CANDIDATE.

Draw a picture of the winner.

VOTE Won in: ☐ CLOSE ELECTION   ☐ LANDSLIDE VICTORY
check one

Winner was born in _____ on _____ .
state   date

An interesting fact about the

candidate: _____

_____

DRAW A CAMPAIGN BUTTON OF THE WINNER

CANDIDATE _____

Running Mate _____

POLITICAL PARTY

REPUBLICAN   circle one   DEMOCRAT

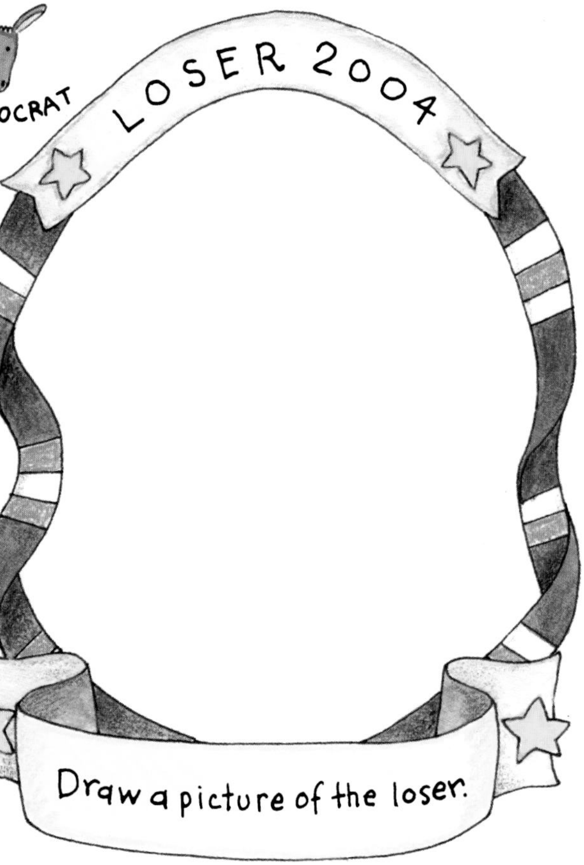

LOSER 2004

WRITE ABOUT THE CANDIDATE.

Draw a picture of the loser.

VOTE   Lost by: ☐ JUST A FEW VOTES ☐ LOTS AND LOTS OF VOTES
check one

Loser was born in _____ on _____ .
state   date

An interesting fact about the candidate: _____

_____

DRAW A CAMPAIGN BUTTON OF THE LOSER

the White House

Who lives at 1600 Pennsylvania Avenue, Washington D.C.?
The president of course! That's the address of the White House! Every president (except for George Washington) has lived in the White House. Our second president, John Adams, moved in on November 1, 1800. (It still wasn't finished.) Over the past 200 years, there have been many changes in the White House, from running water to electricity to its first computers. Now, there is a swimming pool, movie theater, elevators, and even a bowling alley. More than just a house, it is a symbol of the presidency and the United States of America.

Private family quarters

The president's Oval Office is in the WEST WING

State Dining Room

Red Room

Blue

Press Room

Map Room

Diplomatic

The South Lawn has seen lots of activities.

Since 1878- Easter Egg Roll

National Christmas Tree Lighting

The North Side from Pennsylvania Avenue

The South Side

Lincoln's Bedroom and Sitting Room

The East Room has been the scene of many important ceremonies and functions, including weddings and funerals. The Union soldiers camped here during the Civil War.

Green Room

East Room

EAST WING

Room

Reception Room

China Room

Vermeil Room

The White House gets over six million letters a year!

US Mail

Bush played horseshoes.

Carter hosted barbecues.

VICE PRESIDENTS

THEY'RE ONLY "A HEARTBEAT AWAY" FROM THE PRESIDENCY!

The vice president takes over if the president dies or resigns or cannot continue the job. It's the second highest office after the presidency, but many people, including some former vice presidents, don't consider it much of a job.

FDR'S VICE PRESIDENT FOR HIS FIRST TWO TERMS WAS "CACTUS JACK" GARNER.

THE VICE PRESIDENT IS JUST A WAITING BOY, WAITING JUST IN CASE SOMETHING HAPPENS TO THE PRESIDENT.

HE ALSO SAID THAT THE JOB WAS "NOT WORTH A PITCHER OF WARM SPIT."

Here are the vice presidents who took over when the president died or resigned–JOHN TYLER, MILLARD FILLMORE, ANDREW JOHNSON, CHESTER ARTHUR, THEODORE ROOSEVELT, CALVIN COOLIDGE, HARRY S. TRUMAN, LYNDON JOHNSON, and GERALD FORD.

Here are the vice presidents who later got elected president on their own–JOHN ADAMS, THOMAS JEFFERSON, MARTIN VAN BUREN, CALVIN COOLIDGE, HARRY S. TRUMAN, LYNDON JOHNSON, RICHARD NIXON, and GEORGE BUSH.

You usually don't hear much about the vice presidents who never got to be president, like–ELBRIDGE GERRY, HANNIBAL HAMLIN, SCHUYLER COLFAX, CHARLES CURTIS, and many others.

THE VICE PRESIDENT'S HOUSE IS ON THE GROUNDS OF THE U.S. NAVAL OBSERVATORY IN WASHINGTON, D.C.

FIRST LADIES

The president's wife is called the first lady. Their family is called the first family. And sometimes a pet is called the first dog or first cat. First ladies don't get elected, and they don't get a salary, but most of them work very hard. They represent the country. They campaign for their husbands. They take charge of the White House. And they often work for a special cause—like "Say No to Drugs," or the environment.

SOX CLINTON
FIRST CAT

MOST FIRST LADIES HAVE ENJOYED THEIR JOB. BUT SOME, LIKE JANE PIERCE, HATED IT. WHEN SHE HEARD THAT HER HUSBAND HAD BEEN NOMINATED, SHE FAINTED.

Eleanor Roosevelt was one of the greatest women in American history. As first lady, she traveled around the country and the world to help the poor and end racism. She also gave radio talks and wrote books, magazine articles, and a newspaper column.

AFTER FDR DIED, SHE BECAME THE U.S. DELEGATE TO THE UNITED NATIONS.

UNITED STATES

 First ladies are celebrities. Jackie Kennedy was as glamorous and as famous as a movie star.

When a woman is elected president, will her husband be the "first man"?

The Presidents' Kids

George Washington was the father of our country, but he didn't have children of his own. (He did adopt Martha's children.) Practically all presidents have had a family; however, most of the children were already grown by the time their fathers took office. In fact, only 12 children were 12 years old or younger when their fathers were in the White House. The only baby born to a president while he served was Esther Cleveland. President John Adams's son John Quincy Adams became president, and President George Bush's son George W. Bush became president. President William Henry Harrison was the grandfather of President Benjamin Harrison.

Sometimes the children of presidents got into trouble at the White House. Theodore Roosevelt had six children who were nicknamed the White House Gang by the press because they were wild.

Amy Carter had a tree house on the White House grounds. That wouldn't be allowed now. It wouldn't be considered safe. Now children of the president have secret service agents with them all the time.

John F. Kennedy's children, John Jr. and Caroline, sometimes had hamburgers served to them on a silver tray.

WHY IT'S FUN TO BE PRESIDENT

 1. You would have your own movie theater in the White House.

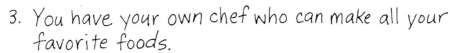

2. You fly on your own private airplane. (Air Force One)

3. You have your own chef who can make all your favorite foods.

 4. You live in a big, beautiful house. (The White House)

 5. You have your own library with over 2,700 books in it.

 6. You can entertain 140 friends in the State Dining Room.

 7. You can bowl in the White House bowling alley anytime you want.

 8. If you get tired of bowling, you can go swimming in your own pool.

 9. You can travel all over the world and meet many interesting people.

 10. You are the most famous person in the country.

CAN A PRESIDENT GET FIRED?

The answer is YES. If the House of Representatives thinks the president did something very wrong, they can IMPEACH him. "Impeach" means the same thing as "accuse."

If the House of Representatives votes to impeach the president, then there is a trial in the Senate. The judge in this trial is the chief justice of the Supreme Court. If the Senate votes GUILTY, then the president must leave his job, and the vice president takes over.

Two presidents have been impeached— Andrew Johnson in 1868, and Bill Clinton in 1998. Both were found not guilty, so they got to stay in office.

One president resigned because he knew he was going to be impeached, and found guilty. This was Richard Nixon, in 1974.

PRESIDENTS IN RETIREMENT

Retired presidents often get lots of work writing books, making speeches, and campaigning for other politicians. But sometimes they just want to live quietly with their families, and enjoy things that ordinary people do.

GEORGE WASHINGTON RETURNED TO MOUNT VERNON, HIS HOME IN VIRGINIA.

NICE AND PEACEFUL HERE.

John Quincy Adams became a congressman. Andrew Johnson became a senator. Ulysses S. Grant wrote a best-selling book about his life.

William Taft was the only president to later be appointed chief justice of the Supreme Court. He said he enjoyed it more than being president.

TAFT

James Polk died only three months after he left the White House. John Tyler had seven more children with his second wife. (He had 15 altogether.)

JIMMY CARTER HELPED TO BUILD AFFORDABLE HOUSING FOR POOR PEOPLE, AND WON THE NOBEL PEACE PRIZE.

STATES WHERE PRESIDENTS WERE BORN

STATES WHERE NO PRESIDENTS WERE BORN

WASHINGTON

Mt. St. Helens

MONTANA

NORTH DAKOTA

Cascade Mountains

OREGON

IDAHO

Yellowstone National Park

WYOMING

SOUTH DAKOTA

NEBRASKA

Gerald Ford

Six presidents were named JAMES.

JAMES

CALIFORNIA

NEVADA

Hoover Dam

Great Salt Lake

UTAH

Rocky Mountains

COLORADO

KANSAS

Eight presidents were born in log cabins.

Richard Nixon

Grand Canyon

ARIZONA

NEW MEXICO

Ok

TEXAS

Dwight
Lyndon

ALASKA

Mount McKinley

HAWAII

You can see that hardly any presidents were born in the western half of the country.

PRESIDENTS BORN?

Ulysses S. Grant
Rutherford B. Hayes
James Garfield
Benjamin Harrison
William McKinley
William H. Taft
Warren G. Harding

Chester A. Arthur
Calvin Coolidge

Franklin Pierce

John Adams
John Quincy Adams
John F. Kennedy
George Bush (Sr.)

George W. Bush

Martin Van Buren
Millard Fillmore
Theodore Roosevelt
Franklin D. Roosevelt

Grover Cleveland

George Washington
Thomas Jefferson
James Madison
James Monroe
William H. Harrison
John Tyler
Zachary Taylor
Woodrow Wilson

James K. Polk
Andrew Johnson

Andrew Jackson

MINNESOTA

MICHIGAN

WISCONSIN

MICHIGAN

NEW YORK

MAINE

VT

NH

MASS

CT

NJ

MD

DEL

PENNSYLVANIA
James Buchanan

IOWA
Herbert Hoover

ILLINOIS
Ronald Reagan

INDIANA

OHIO

WEST VIRGINIA

KENTUCKY
Abraham Lincoln

VIRGINIA

MISSOURI
Harry S. Truman

ARKANSAS
Bill Clinton

TENNESSEE

MISSISSIPPI

NORTH CAROLINA

SOUTH CAROLINA

GEORGIA
Jimmy Carter

ALABAMA

LOUISIANA

FLORIDA

...hower ...on

Virginia is called the "Mother of Presidents" because eight were born there. Ohio comes in second with seven presidents,

63

BIBLIOGRAPHY

Here is a list of books we used
for our report:

The American Heritage Book of the Presidents and Famous Americans edited by Kenneth W. Leish (published by American Heritage Publishing Company)

Don't Know Much About the Presidents by Kenneth C. Davis (published by HarperCollins)

Lives of the Presidents: Fame, Shame (and What the Neighbors Thought) by Kathleen Krull (published by Harcourt Brace)

The New Big Book of U.S. Presidents by Marc Frey and Todd Davis (published by Running Press)

Presidents (Eyewitness Books) by James Barber and John Hareas (published by Dorling Kindersley)

The Smithsonian Book of the First Ladies edited by Edith P. Mayo (published by Henry Holt and Company)

So You Want to Be President? by Judith St. George (published by Philomel Books)

Stuck on the Presidents by Lara Bergen, Lisa Hopp, and Angela Tung (published by Grosset & Dunlap)

To the Best Of My Ability: The American Presidents edited by James M. McPherson (published by Dorling Kindersley)

★ ★ ★ ★ ★ ★ ★ ★ ★ ★ ★ ★